Revival

Youth Study Book

Revival

Faith as Wesley Lived It

Revival: Faith as Wesley Lived It
978-1-426-77884-1   *Also available as an eBook*

Revival: Faith as Wesley Lived It—Large Print Edition
978-1-630-88294-5

Revival: DVD
978-1-426-77682-3

Revival: Leader Guide
978-1-426-77883-4   *Also available as an eBook*

Revival: Youth Study Book
978-1-426-78868-0   *Also available as an eBook*

Revival: Children's Leader Guide
978-1-426-78871-0

For more information, visit www.AdamHamilton.org.

Also by Adam Hamilton

24 Hours That Changed the World

Christianity and World Religions

Christianity's Family Tree

Confronting the Controversies

Enough

Final Words from the Cross

Forgiveness

Leading Beyond the Walls

Love to Stay

Making Sense of the Bible

Not a Silent Night

Seeing Gray in a World of Black and White

Selling Swimsuits in the Arctic

The Journey

The Way

Unleashing the Word

When Christians Get It Wrong

Why?

ADAM HAMILTON

Author of *The Way* and *The Journey*

Revival

FAITH AS WESLEY LIVED IT

YOUTH STUDY BOOK

by Josh Tinley

Abingdon Press / Nashville

REVIVAL: FAITH AS WESLEY LIVED IT
Youth Study Book

This book is printed on elemental chlorine-free paper.

ISBN 978-1-426-78868-0

14 15 16 17 18 19 20 21 22 23—10 9 8 7 6 5 4 3 2

MANUFACTURED IN THE UNITED STATES OF AMERICA

Contents

Introduction

Whether or not you've spent much time in a church that has "Methodist" or "Wesleyan" in its name, you may have heard the name John Wesley. Wesley was the founder of Methodism, and his teachings and example had an influence on dozens of Christian denominations and traditions, including The United Methodist Church, the Church of the Nazarene, the African Methodist Episcopal Church, Churches of God, and the Salvation Army.

Though many denominations consider John Wesley their founder and look to his teachings for wisdom and guidance, Wesley himself never intended to start a new church. He was an ordained priest in the Church of England in the 1700s who devoted his life to reviving Christianity in England and the British colonies. Wesley felt that many of his fellow English Christians were sleepwalking through their faith and needed to be awakened.

As a part of this revival, John Wesley traveled over 250,000 miles, preached thousands of sermons, crossed the Atlantic, and spent time among persons who were despised or ignored by most in England. Though many in the Church of England mocked his enthusiasm, drove him out of their communities, and threatened him with physical violence, thousands of others were eager to hear Wesley's sermons and to join one of his religious societies.

These people, who were the first Methodists, made a social and spiritual impact on England and the American colonies that endures to this day.

For those of us who call ourselves Methodists or count ourselves as John Wesley's theological descendants, revival is in our spiritual DNA. For those of us who aren't part of a Methodist or Wesleyan church, we still have much to learn from John Wesley's life and ministry. Much as Wesley sought to awaken eighteenth-century England from its spiritual slumber, we are called to be alarm clocks in our communities, alerting our fellow Christians to the truth of God's grace and our call to live our lives in service of God and neighbor.

Don't Get Stuck in the 1700s

This Youth Study Book is based on Adam Hamilton's book and program *Revival: Faith as Wesley Lived It*. In the study, you will get to know John Wesley. You'll learn about the time he nearly died in a house fire; you'll get to see him during his college years; you'll watch him fail miserably in Georgia; you'll go to the prayer meeting where Wesley felt his heart "strangely warmed"; you'll join his ministry to coal miners and his crusade against the slave trade. You will also become familiar with John Wesley's teachings on grace, salvation, and justice.

But don't get stuck in the 1700s. This isn't a history textbook. Rather it is a challenge to pursue sanctification, embrace social holiness, and lead a revival of your own in the twenty-first century. The lessons we can learn from John Wesley's teachings, example, and mistakes are as relevant today as they were 250 years ago.

As you work through this book, whether with a group or on your own, consider your relationship with God and the needs of your community. Reflect on how God's grace is at work in your life and on what you can learn from mistakes you've made. Most importantly, focus on what God is calling you to do and on what commitments you might make in response to all you learn and experience in this study.

Using This Resource

(handwritten: we have this if you want it)

This Youth Study Book is designed as a group study but can also be used for personal reading and devotion. As part of the study, some groups may want to use the adult-level DVD, in which Adam Hamilton travels around England to explore the locations and ministry of Wesley.

Each session of the Youth Study Book begins with a chapter for individual reading. People using this study can read these chapters on their own or the group can set aside time for personal reading during the meetings. Sessions also include a variety of activities and discussion prompts for groups. Every session includes:

1. Bible Study: This section includes an activity and discussion prompts related to a key Scripture in that session. Each of these Scriptures was influential in John Wesley's life and teachings.
2. Word Study: This section explores a key term that is important to that session. It looks at definitions of the term and considers how the term helps us understand John Wesley's ministry and teaching as well as our relationships with Christ today.

(handwritten: use what you prefer)

The remaining activities vary according to the session. Some involve reading and discussion, while others involve launching large-scale projects that will require follow-up. Many activities refer to particular sections in the chapter. It may be beneficial to read aloud the corresponding sections while you are working on an activity.

Several activities invite participants to reflect on personal goals, feelings, and experiences and discuss these with a partner or small group. It is essential that all those participating in this study treat their fellow participants with love and respect. Any personal information that becomes known during group discussion is confidential and should be received without judgment.

Enjoy getting to know John Wesley, and one another, as you work through this book. Embrace opportunities to better understand God's love and grace and to respond by leading a revival in your heart and your community.

Session 1 – March 12
Precursors to Revival

"Write this to the angel of the church in Ephesus: . . .

I know your works, your labor, and your endurance. . . . But I have this against you: you have let go of the love you had at first. So remember the high point from which you have fallen. Change your hearts and lives and do the things you did at first."

—Revelation 2:1, 2, 4-5

If you start with the opening chapter of Genesis and read the Bible straight through, you'll notice a couple things right away. First, you'll notice that God calls upon and works through some pretty messed-up people. For instance, "Israel"—the name of God's people—actually comes from a name God gave to Jacob. Jacob, whom we meet in Genesis 25, cheated his brother out of his rightful share of their father's inheritance, cheated his father-in-law out of some

11

choice livestock, and played favorites with his wives and children. Yet Jacob, by God's design, became the father of God's people. Later, we see God work through Moses (a murderer), David (who committed an affair with a married woman and tried to cover it up by having the woman's husband killed), and Mary Magdalene (who was said to have been possessed by seven demons).

Second, you'll notice that God is always working to fix what is broken. You'll see God deliver the people of Israel from slavery in Egypt, then later deliver the people of Judah from exile in Babylon. You'll see God respond with judgment, but also with grace and patience and mercy, when God's people go astray or turn to idols. Most significantly, you'll see God become human in the person of Jesus—defeating death and delivering the world from sin.

These themes—God working through flawed people and God redeeming what is broken—aren't confined to the Bible. We also encounter them throughout the history of the church. Over and over again, God's people fall short of what God wants for us. And over and over again, God finds ways to fix our brokenness, often working through prophets and reformers who have plenty of flaws of their own.

Today there are thousands of Christian denominations around the world, and many of them trace their beginnings to a particular prophet or reformer who called people back to God when they had gone astray. In the Roman Catholic Church, for instance, the Franciscan and Dominican orders are named after Saints Francis and Dominic, respectively. Lutherans trace their heritage to Martin Luther (hence their name), and Calvinist theologians draw from the work of John Calvin. Mennonites are named for their spiritual forebear, Menno Simons.

United Methodists and other Methodists and Wesleyans trace their spiritual lineage back to John Wesley, an eighteenth-century priest in the Church of England. You probably won't find Wesley's name on a list of Christian reformers. He didn't really reform the church the way that Martin Luther or John Calvin did. Those reformers were interested in challenging the church's power structure and doctrines. In that regard, Wesley wasn't really a reformer. He was more of a revivalist.

To revive means to restore to life or to full strength, much as emergency medical personnel might revive a patient who has lost consciousness or had a heart attack. In the church, *revival* refers to a period of spiritual renewal, usually following a period of apathy and decline.

Though John Wesley inspired the founding of many Christian denominations, he never intended to operate outside of the Church of England. Instead of starting a new church, Wesley sought to bring new life and new energy to the church he had dedicated his life to.

Two Centuries of Religious Unrest

John Wesley was born in Epworth, England, on June 17, 1703, to Samuel and Susanna Wesley. Samuel was a priest in the Church of England. He pastored St. Andrew's Church in Epworth, a town in England about 150 miles north of London.

At the time of Wesley's birth, Europe—and England in particular—had spent almost two centuries mired in religious conflict. The Protestant Reformation began in Germany in 1517 when clergyman Martin Luther published his Ninety-Five Theses, a list of grievances about Roman Catholic religious practices. King Henry VIII, England's ruler at the time, was a staunch Catholic, so the Reformation didn't take hold in the British Isles the way that it did on the European continent. But Henry's loyalty to Catholicism didn't last.

The king clashed with the church in Rome when he sought an annulment—a cancellation—of his marriage to Catherine of Aragon. Catherine had not yet given birth to a male heir; and Henry (who didn't really understand human biology) wanted to leave her and marry his mistress, Anne Boleyn, who he thought would have a better chance of giving him a boy. Catholic Pope Clement VII refused to grant an annulment, so Henry took matters into his own hands. In 1534 he assumed the role of Supreme Head of the church within England, and the Church of England separated from the Catholic Church.

Even after the separation, England was not Protestant in the way that other parts of Europe were Protestant. Henry wasn't a fan of the Reformation and remained committed to much of Catholic teaching and practice. In its early years, the Church of England looked a lot like the Roman Catholic Church. Henry's son Edward embraced Protestantism more than his father had, but his half-sister Mary—who assumed the throne after Edward—was a Catholic who sought to put England back under the authority of the pope. But this move back toward Catholicism was short-lived, ending when Elizabeth I (another of Henry VIII's kids) became queen.

Though Elizabeth's reign is often considered a golden age in England's history, religious tensions remained. Some Anglicans (members of the Church of England) favored Catholicism and embraced Catholic practices and worship styles. Meanwhile other English Christians were sympathetic to the Protestant Reformation and felt that the Church of England had not gone far enough in separating itself from Rome. Many of these Christians, influenced by the teachings of reformer John Calvin, became "Puritans" and split from the Church of England in the late seventeenth century. At the same time, tens of thousands of English settlers—both Puritans and members of the Church of England—had found their way to the British colonies in North America, where they joined a host of other groups who had left Europe for religious reasons.

Meet the Wesleys

John Wesley was born into that world of religious unrest. Although his father, Samuel, was a priest at St. Andrew's Church in Epworth, his mother, Susanna, may be the one who played the biggest role in John's education and spiritual development. Susanna's father was a Puritan minister who defied convention and insisted that his daughter receive a classical education. At the time, such schooling was not usually available to girls.

Susanna shared her father's progressive views and saw to it that her daughters were likewise educated. She taught each of her children, boys and girls, for six hours each day and held family devotions on Sunday afternoons. At one point, while Samuel was on the road, members of St. Andrew's—unsatisfied with the associate minister—came to learn from Susanna. When the associate minister complained, Susanna made her defense, arguing that the Holy Spirit had called and empowered her to lead these meetings, and she wasn't one to disagree with the Holy Spirit.

Susanna was intentional about spending one-on-one time with each of her many children, talking with them and asking questions about their relationship with God. She wrote:

> Our children were taught, as soon as they could speak, the Lord's Prayer, which they were made to say at rising and bed-time constantly, to which as they grew bigger were added a short prayer for their parents, and some collects, a short catechism, and some portion of Scripture, as their memories could bear. They were very early made to distinguish the Sabbath from other days, before they could well speak or go. They were as soon taught to be still at family prayers, and to ask a blessing immediately after, which they used to do by signs before they could kneel or speak.[1]

One particular lesson that John learned from his parents was how to persevere during trying times. The Wesleys were familiar with adversity. Nine of Samuel and Susanna Wesley's children died during childhood. The family was often in debt, with Samuel trying to support a large family on a pastor's salary. And making ends meet wasn't Reverend Wesley's only professional challenge. As a priest, Samuel often felt compelled to take stands on controversial issues. This often put him at odds with members of his church who had differing political views or understandings of Christianity. In one instance, Samuel upset a member of the church to whom he owed money. The parishioner responded by having him put into debtor's prison. Samuel was in jail for three months before the bishop paid for his release. When he wrote to his children from prison, Samuel said that he was in good spirits, because going to jail had given him opportunities to minister to his fellow prisoners.

When John was only five years old, someone from the community set fire to the Wesley's home. (Samuel believed it to have been a member of his congregation.) When the family hurried outside, barely escaping the flames, they discovered that everyone had gotten out safely except for five-year-old John. There was no way to get back into the house to rescue John, so all the family could do was kneel and pray. As they did, one of the townspeople noticed John standing at the window; then one man climbed on top of another and pulled John to safety just before the roof collapsed. John's mother Susanna saw John's rescue as the work of God. Quoting Zechariah 3:2, she called him a "brand plucked from the fire."

Adversity would follow John Wesley into his adult life. As you'll see throughout this study, Methodism in many ways grew out of Wesley's response to turmoil. The story of John Wesley and the Methodists fits into the larger story of God's people. It is a story of brokenness and redemption and a story of flawed people, including Wesley himself. But it is also a story of revival, of new life and new ways of living in response to God's grace.

Session 1 Activities

Bible Study: Revelation 2:1-7

Supplies: Bibles, paper, pens or pencils

Read Revelation 2:1-7. This Scripture is a message from John, the author of Revelation, to the church in Ephesus. It is one of seven letters from the opening chapters of Revelation that John wrote to churches in Asia Minor (current-day Turkey). In his message to the Ephesian Christians, John commended them for their endurance and their rejection of evil. But they also had lost something: They had let go of the love they had once had, and they were in need of revival.

In the spirit of this message to the church in Ephesus, write a similar letter to your congregation. Lift up the things your church is doing well, but also point out ways in which the congregation has gotten off track or could improve. This letter can be completely anonymous and you need not show it to anyone. If you would like to bring your thoughts before the congregation, first discuss your ideas with a member of your pastoral staff.

After all your group members have had time to work on their letters, discuss the following questions:

- What does our congregation do especially well? How do we demonstrate our faith in God? How do we follow Jesus' teachings?
- In what ways could our congregation improve? How has our congregation lost track of what it means to love and serve God and others?
- What role can we (as individuals or as a group) play in reviving the congregation and bringing our church into line with God's will?

Word Study: *Revival*

Supplies: Devices with Internet access (optional)

revival

1. a restoring to life, health, or full strength
2. restoration to good condition
3. a spiritual awakening; a renewed enthusiasm for holiness and doing God's will

Discuss:

*   Where have you encountered the word *revival*?
*   When might a person's faith be in need of revival?
*   When might a congregation or Christian community be in need of revival?

If time permits, do some research on revival meetings. Revival meetings are multiday gatherings conducted by churches to rekindle the faith of believers and to attract new converts. These meetings have their roots in the camp meetings that Protestant groups held on the American frontier in the 1800s. Key figures in the revival movement include Billy Sunday (who was also a Major League Baseball player in the 1880s), Ben M. Bogard, Aimee Semple McPherson, and Billy Graham.

Try to answer the following questions as you research revival meetings:

*   What was the purpose of revival meetings, and what did their organizers hope to accomplish?
*   What does one do at a revival meeting? What is the experience like for someone who is attending?
*   What Christian groups are most associated with revival meetings?
*   What impact have these meetings had on Christianity in the United States?

Spiritual Family Tree

Supplies: A markerboard or large sheet of paper, markers, materials for making an artistic representation of a tree (such as markers, crayons, construction paper, paint, wood and building supplies, and/or materials you might find at a craft or hobby store).

As a group, create a spiritual family tree. This tree will pay homage to all the people who—through their love, wisdom, and example—have shaped you spiritually, as individuals and as a group. Begin by making a list of these spiritually influential people. This list may include members of your congregation, family members, or influential Christians throughout history.

Once you have a list, create a tree. You could do this with markers or crayon on posterboard; you could make a tree by cutting paper; you could even paint it on a wall or (if you have the appropriate tools, safety equipment, and supervision) build it out of wood. On each branch of your tree, write the name of one of the persons you named as a spiritual influence. If possible, leave room on your tree to add branches in the coming weeks, months, and years. Display this "spiritual family tree" in your meeting space or put it on display elsewhere in your church building.

Faces of the Reformation

Supplies: One device with Internet access for every three or four people, pens or pencils, paper

Divide into groups of three or four. Each group should have a device with Internet access (smartphone, tablet, laptop, and so on).

To understand John Wesley, we must understand the theological landscape of the world into which he was born. To do that, each group should do some Internet research on a Christian thinker and/or leader who had a substantial impact on John Wesley's world, and whose impact we still feel today. Questions are provided to guide your research. (It's fine if one group researches more than one person or if multiple groups research the same person.)

Martin Luther

- When and where did Martin Luther live and work?
- Why and how did Martin Luther challenge the Roman Catholic Church?
- Why was the doctrine of justification by faith alone so important to Luther?
- What were Luther's views on the Bible?
- How did Luther influence John Wesley?

Henry VIII

- When and where did Henry VIII live?
- What impact did Henry VIII have on the history of the church?
- Why did Henry separate the English church from the Roman Catholic Church?
- How did Henry's actions shape the world in which John Wesley lived (eighteenth-century England)?

John Calvin

- When and where did John Calvin live and work?
- Why did Calvin break from the Roman Catholic Church?
- Calvin is known as a reformer. In what ways did Calvin reform the church?
- What teachings and doctrines is Calvin known for?
- For what reasons did John Wesley disagree with Calvin?

Jacob Arminius

- When and where did Jacob Arminius live?
- How did Arminius disagree with Calvinists?
- What is "preventing grace" or "prevenient grace"?
- How did Arminius influence John Wesley's thinking?

Word to Your Mother

Supplies: Bibles

Read 2 Timothy 1:3-7. Paul, in these verses he wrote to his protégé Timothy, mentions that Timothy's faith was present in his mother and grandmother. Discuss the following questions as a group:

- Who are your "Lois" and "Eunice"? What family members or other adults have been instrumental in shaping your faith?
- What did you learn, either from their words or from their example?
- What do you have in common with these people? How might others see these people in you?

Divide into pairs or groups of three. In your pairs or groups, determine ways that each person can thank or honor the adults who have shaped her or his faith. For persons who are living, a letter or card would be a great way to express gratitude. For persons who have died, a poem or a donation in their honor to a ministry or other charity may be appropriate.

Wrap Up

Review the key points from this session:

- The story of God's people is a story of brokenness and redemption. God often works through flawed people to restore and revive.
- John Wesley was born into a world that had been through two centuries of religious turmoil. He was the son of a priest in the Church of England. John Wesley didn't seek to reform his church or start a new denomination. Rather, he was interested in revival.
- Wesley's parents, and especially his mother, played a big role in shaping his faith. God often uses family members and other adults in our lives to nudge us toward a relationship with Christ.

Session 2 - March 19
A Longing for Holiness

Therefore, once you have your minds ready for action and you are thinking clearly, place your hope completely on the grace that will be brought to you when Jesus Christ is revealed. Don't be conformed to your former desires, those that shaped you when you were ignorant. But, as obedient children, you must be holy in every aspect of your lives, just as the one who called you is holy. It is written, You will be holy, because I am holy.

—1 Peter 1:13-16

If you've learned about John Wesley—whether in confirmation classes, your pastor's sermons, or elsewhere—you probably know him as a preacher, a church leader, a missionary, and a theologian. All of these descriptions are accurate, but perhaps another word better sums up Wesley's life and work: _teacher_.

John Wesley began his studies at Oxford University when he was seventeen and stayed until he was thirty-two. The length of time he spent in college wasn't the result of too much partying and not enough studying. Rather, it was the product of a <u>devotion to</u> academics and learning. Wesley studied at Christ Church College, one of the colleges at Oxford University, earning bachelor's and master's degrees. (If you have seen the *Harry Potter* films, you've seen Christ Church, as parts of the campus were used as locations at Hogwarts in those movies.) After completing his degrees, Wesley was elected as a fellow of Lincoln College, another of Oxford's colleges. He remained a fellow at Lincoln for much of the rest of his life.

At Oxford, Wesley was a good student; he was also, in many ways, a typical student. He enjoyed going to the coffee house and playing games and sports with his fellow students. Wesley assumed that he would go into a career as a teacher or professor, but his parents had other plans for him. They wanted him to go into the family business and be ordained as a priest. Because John's parents, and especially his mother, had such a strong influence on him, Wesley began his preparation for ordination shortly after he graduated.

As he prepared for the priesthood, Wesley came to embrace the vocation that his parents had chosen for him. He drew inspiration from a 1650 book by Jeremy Taylor titled *The Rule and Exercises of Holy Living*. Taylor found guidance in 1 Corinthians 10:31, where Paul says, "Whether you eat or drink or whatever you do, you should do it all for God's glory." That idea of devoting every aspect of one's life to the glory of God was very important to John Wesley. He came to see every moment of every day as an opportunity to grow in love and service of God.

The word *enthusiasm* comes from the Greek words *en theos*, meaning "filled with God." In John Wesley's day, however, the word *enthusiast* wasn't a compliment. It described someone who was passionate about something, but not necessarily in a good way. John's younger brother Charles Wesley, who would follow him to Oxford, noticed that being enthusiastic— being filled with God—didn't win him many friends on campus. At one point, while Charles was at Oxford and John had returned to Epworth, Charles wrote to his older brother, saying that if students were serious about pursuing the Christian faith at Oxford they would receive no small amount of ribbing.

Many of the Wesleys' peers at Oxford believed in God and considered themselves Christians. Plenty of them were good people who tried to live a good and righteous life. But John Wesley felt that the Christian life demanded much more.

Ongoing Restoration Projects

Have you ever fixed up an old car or bike or computer? These days, many of the items we buy aren't meant to last for more than a few years. We're used to replacing phones and tablets every couple years; and we usually don't see much use in restoring old electronics and appliances because we know that it won't be long before something new and better comes along. But if you've ever had the opportunity to take something that is old, worn, or broken and restore it to good working condition, you know the satisfaction and excitement that come from making something new again.

Wesley saw the Christian life as an ongoing restoration project. Each of us was created in God's image. But sin distorts that perfect image. Jesus takes us and makes us new again. Spiritual disciplines such as prayer, reading and studying Scripture, worship, and serving others in Christian love—all of which Wesley referred to as means of grace—are tools that Jesus uses to make us holy.

One particular passage from Scripture informed John Wesley's understanding of holiness. This Scripture, 1 Peter 1:13-16, says,

> Therefore, once you have your minds ready for action and you are thinking clearly, place your hope completely on the grace that will be brought to you when Jesus Christ is revealed. Don't be conformed to your former desires, those that shaped you when you were ignorant. But, as obedient children, you must be holy in every aspect of your lives, just as the one who called you is holy. It is written, *You will be holy, because I am holy.*

In his pursuit of holiness, Wesley became obsessed with discipline. He understood that he was broken and in need of redemption, and he sought to emulate Christ in everything he did.

The Perfect Game

In baseball, have you ever seen a pitcher who was working on a perfect game? In a perfect game, a pitcher faces exactly twenty-seven batters and records twenty-seven outs. No batter gets on base, whether by a hit, a walk, or a fielding error. Since 1900, Major League baseball teams have played more than 180,000 games. Each of those games has featured two teams and thus two opportunities for a pitcher to record a perfect game. That's a total of 360,000 chances for perfection. Only twenty of those 360,000 opportunities have been perfect. That's one occurrence out of about 18,000 attempts.[2]

Because perfect games are so rare, they can be very tense. When a pitcher enters the sixth or seventh inning and still has not allowed a runner to reach base, his teammates often refuse to talk about the fact that a perfect game is in play. Often they don't talk to the pitcher at all. Many in the crowd are unsure of how to react: They want to celebrate the pitcher's great performance, but they don't want to jinx him or put undue pressure on him.

Striving for perfection can be stressful. Even if you've never had the experience of facing a batter in the ninth inning with a chance to complete a perfect game, you may have felt this stress while trying to break a personal record on a video game, attempting to perform a concert or recital without missing a note, or aiming to get a perfect score on a test.

John Wesley was always striving to throw the perfect game. Like Jeremy Taylor (as mentioned earlier), he found inspiration in 1 Corinthians 10:31, where the Apostle Paul writes, "So, whether you eat or drink or whatever you do, you should do it all for God's glory." John's goal was to devote every waking moment of his life to God's glory.

"Methodist"—It Wasn't a Compliment

In 1729, at age twenty-six, John took a job as a teacher and tutor at Oxford. At the time his younger brother Charles was also at Oxford, finishing a bachelor's degree. Charles and a few of his friends were meeting regularly to study Scripture and to encourage one another in faith. They needed someone to be a guide and mentor, so Charles turned to John. As the facilitator of this small group, John was able to bring together the two roles he had trained for: pastor and teacher.

John, Charles, and the rest of the group became a club devoted to holiness and the pursuit of Christian perfection. Members of the club got into the habit of waking before sunrise each morning for individual prayer and Bible study. They also studied together each day and met weekly in John's study at Lincoln College. As a group, they ministered to prisoners, made visits to people who were sick or homebound, and provided educational instruction to orphans. Several members of this group would become prominent religious leaders in England and elsewhere, including the great evangelist George Whitefield, who would help launch the First Great Awakening in the American colonies and who would later have a profound influence on John Wesley's ministry.

The Wesleys' club become a target of mockery for some of their Oxford peers. Students called the group "Bible moths" or the "Holy Club." They also poked fun at the group's methodical approach to Christian faith, calling them "Methodists."

Methodism began with this "Holy Club" at Oxford, and it adopted a name that was meant as an insult. The original Methodists were enthusiasts who sought nothing less than perfection. Of course, Wesley and his friends weren't perfect. Neither are we. But we can emulate their dedication and their effort to give every aspect of their lives to God.

- Have you ever been called a mean name? Wesley embraced his. I embrace my "nerdy" nature. Don't let people bully you, but think of the good behind these names too.

Session 2 Activities

Bible Study: 1 Peter 1:13-21

Supplies: Bibles

Read 1 Peter 1:13-21, then reread verses 14 and 15. Discuss the following questions:

- What do you think Peter means by "former desires"?
- What are some ideas or priorities that one might set aside when one becomes a Christian?
- What "former desires," ideas, or behaviors have you given up because of your faith? When are you tempted to go back to your old ways of thinking or acting?
- Peter tells his readers to conduct themselves "with reverence" while they are "dwelling in a strange land" (verse 17). What do you think he means by "dwelling in a strange land"? What is "strange" about our world?

When Peter writes in verse 16, "It is written, *You will be holy, because I am holy*," he is referring to the opening verses of Leviticus 19. Read Leviticus 19 in its entirety. That chapter is part of the ancient Israelites' holiness code, which gave God's people specific instructions on every aspect of their lives, even those that seem mundane to twenty-first-century readers. Discuss:

- Which of the rules in this chapter seem reasonable? Which, if any, seem strange to you?
- Why do you think God seemed so concerned with every aspect of the Israelites' lives?
- What does this chapter teach us about holiness? How can you be holy in every aspect of your life?

Word Study: *Holy*

holy
1. sacred
2. devoted to serving God or the church
3. free, by God's grace, from the tendency to commit sin

Discuss:
*   What makes a person or object holy?
*   Who are some people you would consider holy? What makes them holy?

Wesley and the eighteenth-century Methodist movement placed an emphasis on holiness and Christian perfection that remains influential in many Christian traditions and denominations still today, including (among others) Methodist churches, the Church of the Nazarene, Churches of God, and the Salvation Army.

Perfect, as God Is Perfect

Supplies: An indoor child's game such as a bowling set or basketball hoop

In Matthew 5:48 (NRSV) Jesus tells his followers, "Be perfect, therefore, as your heavenly Father is perfect." Hebrews 6:1 (NRSV) challenges us to "go on toward perfection."

To get a feel for what *perfection* means, play an indoor child's game and see if anyone in your group can put together a perfect game. For example, you could use a child's toy bowling set and see if anyone is able to bowl a strike every time. You could use a toy basketball hoop and see if any person is able to hit twenty consecutive free throws. You could use a toy dartboard—one that uses Velcro balls instead of actual darts—and see if any player can hit the bulls-eye on every throw.

After all group members have had a try at perfection, discuss the activity:

- For those of you who were able to complete a perfect game, how difficult was it?
- How much anxiety or pressure did you feel during this activity? Did the pressure seem to increase as the game went on?
- For those of you who were unable to complete a perfect game, how did your approach to the game change after your first mistake? Did you still feel an urgency to be perfect for the remainder of the game? Did you feel as though the pressure had been lifted?
- How does any of this relate to our lives as Christians?

When we strive for Christian perfection, we will likely encounter some anxiety and pressure as well. Being free from the tendency to sin is much more difficult than bowling a perfect game or remaining perfect from the free-throw line. For this reason, the first step toward Christian perfection is admitting that, apart from God's grace, we are incapable of perfection.

Teachers of a Lifetime

Though we often think of him as a preacher and evangelist, John Wesley was also a teacher. And teaching and education have long been important in Methodist and other Wesleyan denominations. Discuss the following questions:

- What is the role of a teacher?
- What makes a teacher a good teacher?

Then consider some of the teachers who have had an impact on your life. After a couple of minutes for reflection, identify two teachers who have influenced you in a particularly meaningful way. One of these persons should be a teacher in a traditional teaching role, such as a school teacher or Sunday school teacher. The other should be someone outside a traditional teaching role who has taught you a great deal or influenced you in an important way.

For traditional teachers, think of one thing they taught you related to their subject matter; then, for both kinds of teachers, think of one thing they taught you that was unrelated to their area of expertise but was still important.

In groups of three or four, talk about the teachers you have selected and the qualities that make or made them good teachers. Make a note of some things these teachers have in common. Also discuss ways that teachers can shape and influence their students (either for good or for bad).

Make an effort in the coming weeks to seek out the teachers you've selected and thank them for what they've done and what they've taught you. You could express thanks in a letter, a short social media message, or a personal visit.

Get in the Habit of Holiness

Supplies: Index cards, pens or pencils

Holiness is not something that a person achieves instantly. One does not simply decide to be holy. Rather, it is an ongoing process, the result of developing habits. And habits are often the product of persistence and long-term commitments.

Think about practices or disciplines you have committed to. For instance, maybe you decided to give up eating a certain type of unhealthy food, or maybe you made a commitment to volunteer with a particular ministry or charity.

Discuss:

- If you made such a commitment, how long were you able to keep it? Has this commitment become a habit?
- What makes commitments difficult to keep?

Decide on a holy habit that you can commit to developing—something you can do each day or week until it becomes a part of your life. Here are some possibilities:

- Commit yourself to service. Volunteer to spend time with residents at a nursing home or an assisted-living facility once a week or month, or tutor elementary schoolchildren who need extra help on their homework.

- Set aside daily devotional time. Allow ten to fifteen minutes each morning or evening to read and reflect on Scripture or a devotional guide and to pray.
- Abstain from something that is unnecessary, harmful, or having a negative effect on your relationship with God. Give up an unhealthy food; eliminate hurtful words from your vocabulary and gossip from your conversations; make a commitment not to spend money on certain items you do not need.

Spend several minutes praying about and reflecting on commitments or holy habits you're considering. When you have decided on your holy habit, write it down on an index card. Then find a partner. Talk to your partner about the commitment you will be making and learn about your partner's commitment. During the coming weeks, hold each other accountable to these commitments, and check in with each other every few days.

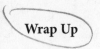

Wrap Up

Before you conclude, review the key points from this session:

- John Wesley spent many years at Oxford University. There he, along with his brother Charles and several of their peers, formed a club devoted to holiness and the pursuit of Christian perfection.
- Wesley was mocked for his enthusiasm and devotion. Oxford students came up with the name "Methodist" as a way to mock Wesley and his friends and their methodical approach to faith.
- Holiness is being completely devoted to loving and serving God and doing all things for God's glory.
- We are all ongoing restoration projects. We were made perfect in God's image. Sin has distorted that image, but—through God's grace—it is being restored.

Session 3 — April 2
A Crisis of Faith

What does the scripture say? Abraham had faith in God, and it was credited to him as righteousness. Workers' salaries aren't credited to them on the basis of an employer's grace but rather on the basis of what they deserve. But faith is credited as righteousness to those who don't work, because they have faith in God who makes the ungodly righteous.

Therefore, since we have been made righteous through his faithfulness combined with our faith, we have peace with God through our Lord Jesus Christ. We have access by faith into this grace in which we stand through him, and we boast in the hope of God's glory.

—Romans 4:3-5; 5:1-2

Wesley was English: He was born in England, went to school in England, taught and preached and wrote in England, and died in England. But when he

33

Went to to Preach
Georgia

was in his early thirties, Wesley crossed the Atlantic to work as a missionary in the American colony of Georgia.

British general, statesman, and philanthropist James Oglethorpe established Georgia in 1732 as a refuge for people who had been thrown into prison because they couldn't pay their debts. He named the colony after King George II. Oglethorpe proposed taking debt prisoners, many of whom were very poor, away from the bad living conditions in British jails and to the New World where they'd get a fresh start. After he established the new colony, along with the coastal city of Savannah, Oglethorpe returned to England with four Native Americans, whom the English called "noble savages."

John Wesley met these "noble savages" in England and decided to travel with Oglethorpe to Georgia to work as a priest in Savannah and as an evangelist to Native Americans. Wesley didn't really like the idea of sailing halfway around the world to be a missionary, especially since he was prone to seasickness. But he was willing to endure the discomfort because he saw an opportunity to score points with the Almighty.

A Holy Disaster

He was trying to live it

Holy but Death seem imminent

had fear

The trip from England to Georgia was trying for Wesley not only because of his tendency to get seasick but also because of the storms he encountered. The storms were both weather-related and spiritual. When the weather got rough, John grew afraid. But he noticed a group of Christians on board who had no fear of the storms. These Christians, who were Moravians (a German denomination inspired by the teachings of late-fourteenth-century reformer Jan Hus), sang hymns even as the weather threatened to sink the ship. Wesley was impressed by the Moravians' faith but was bothered that he didn't share their confidence in the face of disaster. He had devoted so much of his life to holiness and righteousness, yet he wasn't at peace when death seemed imminent.

After a harrowing three months at sea, Wesley disembarked in Savannah, Georgia, bringing with him the fervor for holiness that he had developed at Oxford. Though he became popular as a preacher in Savannah, Wesley's enthusiasm for holy living didn't catch on. Shortly after arriving, he confiscated

Holy living
didn't catch on

all the rum that the ships had brought over from England and destroyed it. This didn't sit well with his fellow colonists. Nor did his 5:00 a.m. prayer services, which church members were required to attend if they wanted to receive Holy Communion.

If you've spent much time reading the Gospels (the first four books of the New Testament, which tell the story of Jesus' life and ministry), you've probably encountered the Pharisees. The Pharisees were members of a Jewish sect that was fiercely devoted to keeping *all* God's commandments. Christians tend to focus on the Ten Commandments, which we find in the books of Exodus and Deuteronomy. But the Bible's first five books contain hundreds of *mitzvot* (commandments)—Jewish tradition later identified 613 in all. Pharisees believed that it was important to follow each and every one.

Many Jewish people in the first century would have regarded the Pharisees as righteous and holy, worthy of reverence and respect. But in the Gospels, the Pharisees usually play the villains. Their dedication to following every letter of the law often caused them to overlook the spirit of the law; as a result, they ended up griping when Jesus healed on the sabbath, and they tried to trap Jesus with tricky legal questions.

In many ways John Wesley had become the eighteenth-century Christian version of a Pharisee. He was obsessed with being the perfect follower of Christ and expected his parishioners to share his obsession. They didn't, and some of them resented their new pastor. According to Wesley, one member of his church said to him, "I like nothing you do. . . . Indeed there is neither man nor woman in the town who minds a word you say."[3]

Romance Gone Bad

Meanwhile Wesley found himself embroiled in a romance with a young woman in his church named Sophia Hopkey. At the time she was seventeen or eighteen and looking for a husband. (That's how things worked back then.) Wesley was attracted to Sophia, as she was to him, but he had a bit of a problem. As a part of his commitment to holiness, Wesley had promised God that he would never marry. At first, Sophia was so enamored with John that she was fine with this arrangement. She was willing to commit to a lifelong relationship that didn't involve marriage or physical affection or romance. But Sophia eventually decided that she needed something more and began dating another man.

Word came to Wesley that Sophia would marry her new love interest unless John were to intervene. But Wesley would not waver from his commitment to celibacy—not even for Sophia. Instead, he decided to fight back. He accused Sophia of dating two men at the same time, even though John and Sophia were never actually dating. Then he went a step further and told her that she could not receive Holy Communion until she repented of her wrongdoing. Sophia, knowing she had not actually done anything wrong, called John's bluff. When she came forward to receive Communion, John—in front of the entire congregation—refused her.

John didn't get away with this little stunt. Sophia married the man she'd been dating, and her new husband brought up Wesley on charges of defamation of character. John was arrested but released without bail until his trial. Though he avoided spending time in jail, his antics drove away his parishioners, and church attendance dropped.

The authorities in Georgia ordered Wesley not to leave the colony, but John disobeyed the order. While he was awaiting trial, he sneaked into the Carolinas, then boarded a ship back to England. He had failed. He had not been a successful evangelist to the native peoples in Georgia; the members of his church had rejected him; and his romantic endeavors had ended in disaster.

Wesley's experience in Georgia was discouraging and humbling. He became aware of his shortcomings and of the fact that he could not achieve perfection on his own.

Strangely Warmed

Here's a bit of trivia: What is the most common street name in the United States?

The answer? "Second." According to the most recent geographic data (which is from 1993, so things may be a little different now), there are nearly 11,000 streets, roads, and avenues in the United States named "Second."

("First" is third on the list, with just under 10,000.) There are millions of streets in the United States alone. But other than the streets that seem to pop up in every city—such as "Second" and "First" and "Main" and "Park"—there aren't many streets whose names are widely known and recognized.[4]

In the United States we have a handful of famous streets that we associate with the cities they're in. There's Beale Street in Memphis, Bourbon Street in New Orleans, Lombard Street in San Francisco, Park Avenue in New York, and Hollywood Boulevard in Los Angeles. Paris has the Champs-Élysées, Barcelona has La Rambla, and London has Downing Street and Abbey Road. For Christians influenced by John Wesley, there's another London Street with a familiar name: Aldersgate Street.

On the evening of May 24, 1738, John Wesley reluctantly attended a religious society meeting on Aldersgate Street. Religious societies were similar to the small groups that meet in many churches today. They met regularly to study Scripture and to encourage one another to grow in faith. This particular religious society was studying a commentary that reformer Martin Luther had written on Romans.

To this point in his life, Wesley had been obsessed with pleasing God. He had an understanding of holiness that involved following all the rules and working to earn God's favor. This approach to his faith made his debacle in Georgia especially disheartening. Wesley felt as though he'd failed to please God.

But Wesley heard and experienced something at the meeting on Aldersgate Street that gave him a new perspective. He later wrote:

> In the evening I went very unwillingly to a society in Aldersgate Street, where one was reading Luther's Preface to the Epistle to the Romans. About a quarter before nine, while he was describing the change which God works in the heart through faith in Christ, I felt my heart strangely warmed. I felt I did trust in Christ, Christ alone for salvation; and an assurance was given me that he had taken away *my* sins, even *mine*, and saved *me* from the law of sin and death.[5]

This moment on Aldersgate Street was a conversion experience for Wesley. It may seem strange that someone who had been a Christian his entire life, an ordained priest in the Church of England, and the leader of a club devoted to Christian holiness could be "converted." But this moment changed Wesley's entire understanding of God's grace and how we relate to God. To this point in his life, Wesley had lived as though salvation was something that he had to earn by following rules and doing good works. But following this meeting on Aldersgate Street, he lived with the confidence that God's grace alone would save him.

The idea that one is saved by grace rather than by works was not new to Wesley. He was well schooled in the Bible and Christian theology, and he understood—on an intellectual level—that God's grace through Christ was responsible for our salvation. But Wesley had been living as though his salvation depended on impressing God or scoring points for righteousness. After Aldersgate, his approach to faith changed. He was no longer bound by rules and high expectations. Instead he was free to live as one loved and accepted by God.

Those meeting on Aldersgate Street that evening were reading Martin Luther's preface to Romans. In Romans the Apostle Paul writes:

> What does the scripture say? *Abraham had faith in God, and it was credited to him as righteousness.* Workers' salaries aren't credited to them on the basis of an employer's grace but rather on the basis of what they deserve. But faith is credited as righteousness to those who don't work, because they have faith in God who makes the ungodly righteous.

> Therefore, since we have been made righteous through his faithfulness combined with our faith, we have peace with God through our Lord Jesus Christ. We have access by faith into this grace in which we stand through him, and we boast in the hope of God's glory. (Romans 4:3-5; 5:1-2)

In this passage, Paul goes all the way back to Abraham to make the point that God saves us by grace through faith; we don't work for our salvation. Abraham didn't do anything to earn God's favor. God's favor was available to Abraham, and he needed only to accept it.

John Wesley now knew that he could not win his salvation by being holy, but that didn't mean that holiness and good works were no longer important. After Aldersgate, he understood that holiness was not about impressing God; it was a response to God's gift of salvation.

Session 3 Activities

Bible Study: Romans 4:3-5; 5:1-11
Supplies: Bibles, a markerboard or paper, markers, index cards, pens or pencils

Read Romans 4:3-5; 5:1-11. Also reread the sections of this study called "A Holy Disaster" and "Strangely Warmed." Then discuss:

* Who is Abraham, and why is he so important? (You might look at Genesis 12:1-3 and Genesis 17:1–8.)
* Why, according to Paul (the author of Romans), was Abraham righteous? What role did Abraham play in being made righteous? What role did God play?
* Why, according to Paul, do we have peace with God? Do you feel at peace with God? Why or why not?

Reread Romans 5:3-5. List some of John Wesley's problems. Talk about how each of these problems produced endurance, character, and hope.

Jot down, on one side of an index card, some of the problems you are currently dealing with. Then, on the other side, copy Romans 5:3-5. Keep this card in your wallet, purse, or Bible as a reminder that, because of God's grace, you have hope, even in trying times.

Word Study: *Righteous*

righteous
1. good, upright, and moral
2. morally right
3. slang: great, wonderful

Discuss:

- What comes to mind when you hear the words *righteous* or *righteousness*?
- Whom would you consider "righteous"? Why?
- *Righteousness* could be defined as "being made right." How are we "made right" by God's grace? Can we make ourselves right?
- Read the "Strangely Warmed" section from this session. What did John Wesley learn about righteousness at the meeting on Aldersgate Street?

Dreams Come True

Supplies: Paper, pens or pencils, markers or colored pencils

When you were a small child, did you have dreams or expectations of what life would be like when you became a teenager? On a sheet of paper, draw or write about the dreams you had for yourself when you were younger. Show your drawing or description to a partner. Discuss with your partner:

- What dreams have come true for you?
- In what ways has your teenage life fallen short of your dreams?
- In what ways has your teenage life been even better than you could have dreamed?

Chances are that you have dreams and expectations now about what life will be like when you're an adult. Regardless of how hard you work or how passionate you are about your goals, it's almost certain that some of your dreams and aspirations won't come to fruition. It's also quite possible that you'll end up having your dream job or going to your dream school only to discover that it falls short of your expectations.

That's what happened to John Wesley. His trip to Georgia didn't go as planned. In fact, it was a disaster. But shortly after he returned home he had an experience at Aldersgate that gave him a new perspective on life. His plans and his dreams no longer mattered so much. What mattered was becoming the person God had created and called him to be.

Spend some time in silent prayer reflecting on God's plans for you. What do you know about whom God has created you to be and what God has called you to do? God's plans might not be apparent to you now. But know that God loves you, claims you, and is at work in your life. Be mindful of where God is leading you and be ready to respond.

Give John Wesley Some Relationship Advice
Supplies: Paper, pens or pencils

Those who belong to Methodist and Wesleyan churches often look to John Wesley's sermons and writings for advice on holy living. But during his time in Georgia, Wesley himself would have benefited from advice. Reread the information about Wesley's relationship with Sophia Hopkey from the "Romance Gone Bad" section. In groups of three or four, consider each stage of Wesley and Hopkey's relationship and come up with some advice that you could have given Wesley.

- John and Sophia meet. Each is attracted to the other, but John is committed to celibacy and believes that he should not marry.
- Sophia tells Wesley that, if she cannot marry him, she might also take a vow of celibacy.
- Sophia decides that she really does want to marry. While she would prefer to marry John, she cannot keep waiting for him and begins dating another man.
- Wesley accuses Sophia of being unfaithful and refuses to serve her Holy Communion until she repents.
- Sophia and her husband, William Williamson, file suit against Wesley, claiming that he has defamed Sophia's character. Wesley's reputation suffers and attendance at his church plummets.

After you've given Wesley some relationship advice, discuss:

- What does Wesley's relationship with Sophia Hopkey tell us about who he was at this point in his life?

- What do you think Wesley learned from this experience?
- What does our Christian faith teach us about how we are to live in relationship with other people?
- What does our Christian faith teach us about romantic relationships, including those that don't turn out as we'd like them to?

Strangely Warmed

Supplies: Hot-spiced candies

Think of a time in your life when you felt at peace with your life and with God. It doesn't necessarily need to be a time when everything was going well; it could just be a time when you were certain that everything would work out (even if you didn't know why or how it would work out).

Find a partner. Talk with your partner about this experience. As you discuss, consider the following questions:

- Why did you feel at peace during this time of your life?
- Were there any reasons not to feel at peace during this time? Was anything going on that would have been stressful or frustrating under different circumstances?
- How did you feel God's presence during this time? How was God present through other people?

John Wesley said about his experience on Aldersgate Street on May 24, 1738, "I felt my heart strangely warmed. I felt I did trust in Christ, Christ alone, for salvation; and an assurance was given me that he had taken away *my* sins, even *mine*, and saved *me* from the law of sin and death." The peace Wesley felt that evening was especially powerful. We too have the assurance that Christ has taken away our sins and that we can fully trust Christ for our salvation. This truth should give us some peace, even when our lives feel chaotic.

In honor of Wesley's heart-warming experience, have every person take a spicy piece of candy, such as a red hot. May the heat from this candy be a reminder of the fire of the Holy Spirit that burns within each one of us.

Wrap Up

Before you conclude, review the key points from this session:

- When John Wesley was in his early thirties, he traveled to Georgia with a plan to be an evangelist to the native peoples there.
- Wesley's trip to the American colonies was a disaster, spiritually and romantically. He returned to England dejected.
- On May 24, 1738, Wesley attended a meeting on Aldersgate Street in London. As the group was studying Martin Luther's preface to Romans, John felt his heart "strangely warmed." He understood in a new way that Christ had taken away his sins and that God's grace was sufficient for his salvation.
- Before Aldersgate, Wesley had tried to score points with God by following rules and doing good works. After Aldersgate, Wesley understood that good works didn't earn salvation; they were a response to God's gift of salvation.

Session 4 — April 9
The Necessity of Grace

For by grace you have been saved through faith, and this is not your own doing; it is the gift of God—not the result of works, so that no one may boast. For we are what he has made us, created in Christ Jesus for good works, which God prepared beforehand to be our way of life.

—Ephesians 2:8-10 NRSV

Is there one verse of the Bible that really sticks with you? Is there a verse you have memorized that stays with you or that you recall in difficult situations?

In difficult times, John Wesley had a short Scripture passage that he came back to over and over again: Ephesians 2:8-10. These three verses, which teach that salvation is not something we can earn but a gift from God, were the key text in at least forty of Wesley's sermons.

All people deal with disappointment. We all have had endeavors that didn't work out as we would have liked or even that failed miserably. Disappointment can lead to frustration, and frustration can lead to despair. The antidote for this frustration and despair is hope. And we can find hope in Wesley's favorite

45

verses from Ephesians. The author of these verses, the Apostle Paul, tells us that we cannot save ourselves from the mess we find ourselves in. But God can, and God does.

We know that, in Christ, God has saved us from sin and death, from frustration and despair. But Paul doesn't stop there; God also saves us *for* something. As Paul explains, God saves us for "good works, which God prepared beforehand to be our way of life" (NRSV). This part about good works was as important to Wesley as the part about being "saved through faith." He understood that God's grace does not absolve us from responsibility. We don't get to do whatever we want, knowing that God has already saved us. Rather, God's grace enables us and empowers us to take on a new way of life.

Let's Talk About Grace

If you had to use one word to describe John Wesley's understanding of a Christian's relationship with God, that word would be *grace*. Wesley's views on grace are what set him and his spiritual descendants apart from those who came before. John Wesley understood that God's grace acts on us in three different ways: prevenient, justifying, and sanctifying. One of these expressions of God's grace is acting on us at every moment during our lives.

Prevenient grace is grace that precedes. This is the grace by which God works on us even before we are aware of God's presence. It is the grace that draws us toward God and enables us to accept God's love and forgiveness. We see evidence of prevenient grace in Scripture. For instance, God tells the prophet Jeremiah, "Before I created you in the womb I knew you; before you were born I set you apart" (Jeremiah 1:5). In the Gospel of John, Jesus teaches, "No one can come to me unless they are drawn to me by the Father who sent me" (John 6:44). When we say yes to God, God has already said yes to us.

The belief in prevenient grace is one reason why Methodist and Wesleyan churches practice infant baptism. Though some other Christian traditions only baptize people who are old enough to make an informed decision about their faith, churches in the Wesleyan tradition understand that God is at work in the life of a baby, even though that baby has no idea who God is.

Prevenient grace nudges an individual toward a relationship with God and makes the second movement of grace possible. When a person accepts Christ's gifts of love and forgiveness, she or he experiences *justifying grace*. To justify means to make right. For instance, when you try to justify why you were out past curfew on Friday night, you are hoping to make things right so that you'll stay out of trouble. God made things right through us in the person of Jesus, who died to atone for our sins and then defeated death to give everyone hope for eternal life.

John Wesley experienced God's justifying grace during the meeting on Aldersgate Street on May 24, 1738. This moment of justification was not only the culmination of God's prevenient grace working in John Wesley's life; it also was the beginning of something new. When we are justified, we begin to experience the third movement of God's grace, *sanctifying grace*, and grow toward perfection. To sanctify means to make holy. Sanctifying grace restores us and perfects us. It allows us to love and serve God and others and to become the people God created us to be.

Wesley and the Kingswood Colliers

In previous sessions you learned that many people grew tired of Wesley's enthusiasm. His enthusiasm didn't go away following his experience on Aldersgate Street. If anything he became more zealous, and his critics found him even more annoying. By the end of 1738, only five churches in London would still allow Wesley to preach.

In the spring of 1739, Wesley got a letter from his old Oxford friend George Whitefield. Whitefield had been ministering to coal miners, or colliers, outside of the city of Bristol. Wesley made the 100-mile journey from London to Bristol on horseback and arrived to discover that Whitefield had not been preaching from a pulpit inside a church building. Rather, he'd been preaching outdoors to anyone who was interested in listening. And plenty of people were listening.

John Wesley joined his friend and ministered to coal miners living in an area near Bristol called Kingswood. The colliers who worked in Kingswood's eighty mine pits had rough lives and often died young. The community lacked churches and schools. It wasn't exactly the sort of environment that teachers and preachers liked to work in. So Wesley and Whitefield's witness and presence—and especially their message of free grace—made a big impression on the people of Kingswood. Wesley reported the attendance of 47,500 people who came to hear him preach during his first month in the Bristol area.[6]

When miners and others in Kingswood accepted Christ, Wesley invited them to join small groups called religious societies. It wasn't long before these religious societies could no longer accommodate the large number of people who were interested in joining them. Two of these groups, with Wesley's help, came together to buy some land and build the first Methodist church building. (To be clear, this new congregation belonged to the Church of England and was not part of a separate Methodist denomination.)

This church building in Bristol was called the New Room. It included an upstairs apartment where Wesley lived when he was in Bristol, as well as additional apartments for visiting preachers. It wasn't long before the New Room had become the headquarters of a vibrant and growing Methodist movement.

No Limits

Perhaps Wesley and Whitefield had such an impact on the colliers of Kingswood because grace was at the heart of their message. They emphasized the truth that God loved and was at work in every person. This message contrasted with another popular understanding of salvation. Those who followed the teachings of John Calvin believed that God had selected, or predestined, some of the people—the Elect—for eternal life. Those who were part of the Elect could not resist God's gift of salvation; those who were not a part of this group could not achieve salvation. Calvin and his followers could point to Scriptures to justify these beliefs, but Wesley considered the idea of predestination abhorrent and inconsistent with the life and teachings of Christ. John Wesley felt strongly that God's grace knew no limits. He preached that God's prevenient grace was at work in all people, even those who had no knowledge of God or the church, and that this grace made it possible for anyone

R Grace
rivival

to accept God's gift of salvation. And he preached that God's grace never leaves us but continues to work on us, molding us into the perfect image of Christ.

Wesley not only believed and taught about grace; he also became a personification of it. He traveled throughout England and preached thousands of sermons to bring people the good news of God's grace. Countless people came to know God's love and forgiveness because of the work that John Wesley was doing. But the work didn't stop with Wesley; it extended through the work of the other Methodists. They were bearers of God's grace through their witness and example and through acts of love, mercy, and kindness. They led what we might call a grace revival.

We are all beneficiaries of God's grace. It is because of God's grace that you are reading this book. Regardless of whether you have been a Christian for several years, have recently accepted Christ, or don't yet feel as though you have a relationship with God, you have been touched by grace. As you grow in grace, you—like Wesley and the early Methodists—will feel compelled to bring the good news of salvation to others.

Session 4 Activities

Bible Study: Ephesians 2:8-10
Supplies: Bibles

Think of a celebrity you especially admire. If you were given a chance to meet this person, what would you do to impress him or her? Discuss your ideas with a partner or group of three. Talk about how the celebrity might respond to your attempts. Then discuss:

- What sorts of things do you do to impress or score points with people? Which of these things have worked? Which have been unsuccessful?
- Why do our attempts to impress people sometimes fall short?
- What happens when you try too hard to impress someone?
- What things impress you most about a person?

John Wesley tried to impress God. But his efforts to impress fell short. He later realized he had been going about things the wrong way. Read Ephesians 2:8-10.

- According to the Apostle Paul, the author of these verses, where does our salvation come from?
- What do we have to do to score points with God or earn salvation? *NOTHING*
- Consider what John Wesley went through when he tried to score points with God as an evangelist to Native Americans in Georgia. Why, after what he had been through, do you think these verses were so meaningful to Wesley?
- What sorts of things have you done in the hope of impressing God? When have your efforts to impress God or to be a good Christian fallen flat?
- How do Paul's words in these verses give you hope and comfort?

Often as Christians, we focus on what Christ has saved us *from* (sin and death). The verses from Paul's letter to the Ephesians place the focus on what Christ has saved us *for*.

- What, according to Paul, does Christ save us *for*?
- What do you think it means that we have been created for "good works"?
- What are some good works you've been given the opportunity to perform?

Word Study: *Grace*

grace

1. mercy
2. a gift that is freely given, not earned
3. favor bestowed by a superior or person of authority
4. elegance, beautiful form and movement

Discuss:

- How would you define the word *grace*? Where do you encounter the word?
- What persons would you describe as full of grace? Why?

Read the section called "Let's Talk About Grace" in this session. Then discuss:

- What is "prevenient grace"? Which of the definitions above describes prevenient grace?
- What is "justifying grace"? Which of the definitions above describes justifying grace?
- What is "sanctifying grace"? Which of the definitions above describes sanctifying grace?

A Grace Timeline
Supplies: Paper, assorted art supplies

Read "Let's Talk About Grace" in this session. Then make a timeline of your life, from birth to the present. Beneath the line on your timeline, mark significant moments in your life. These might include the birth of a sibling, getting your driver's license, scoring your first soccer goal, or landing a role in the school play. Above the line, mark ways in which God's grace has been at work in your life.

You could divide the top of your timeline into three sections: prevenient, justifying, and sanctifying. If you were baptized as an infant or young child, you could put this on your timeline as an example of prevenient grace. If you had a moment when you accepted Christ and became a Christian, you could include this as an example of God's justifying grace. (And it's fine if you can't point to a single moment. For many people, accepting Christ is a process.) Your grace timeline might feature events such as being invited to church by a friend or family member, experiencing confirmation, getting the opportunity to lead worship on youth Sunday, or telling your faith story to a friend. You could also add "mountaintop" experiences, where you felt God's presence in a special way. These might include moments at church camp or on mission trips.

Regardless of what you put on your timeline, know that your timeline is still moving forward and that God's grace will continue to have an impact on your life into the future.

Grace in Three Movements
Supplies: Bibles, posterboard and/or large sheets of paper, assorted art supplies

Perhaps no word was more important to John Wesley's understanding of God and the Christian life than *grace*. Wesley saw that Christians experience God's grace in three different ways. First there is prevenient grace, the grace that nudges us toward a relationship with God. Then there is justifying grace, which assures us that our sins are forgiven and we have salvation through Christ.

Finally we experience sanctifying grace, through which we grow in holiness and go on toward Christian perfection.

As a service to your congregation, create a large poster or posters that explain and illustrate these three movements of grace. For each type of grace, provide the following:

- The name: prevenient, justifying, or sanctifying
- The definition: Define each of the three movements of grace.
- An illustration: Give an example of each type of grace. An example of prevenient grace could be an invitation to church by a friend; an example of sanctifying grace might be commitment to a daily prayer regimen.
- A Scripture: Provide a verse or verses from the Bible to support or illustrate each type of grace. Here are some possible Scriptures to choose from:
   - Prevenient grace: Jeremiah 1:5; Ezekiel 34:11-16; Luke 15; John 6:44.
   - Justifying grace: Romans 3:21-26; 2 Corinthians 5:1-5, 21; Galatians 2:16-17.
   - Sanctifying grace: Ephesians 2:8-10; Hebrews 6:1-3; James 2:13-18.

Be the Grace
Supplies: A markerboard or large sheets of paper, markers, slips of paper, pens or pencils

Read the sections "Wesley and the Kingswood Colliers" and "No Limits."

John Wesley and George Whitefield ministered to coal miners outside of Bristol. These people had largely been ignored by other religious leaders, but they also were eager to receive the good news of God's grace. As a group, list on a markerboard groups of people who are often ignored and could benefit from hearing some good news. (Don't list names of specific people.) As a group, select one of the groups on your list and come up with one way that you can show these people that God loves them and that other people care about them. You might visit and bring gifts to people in a nursing home or assisted living facility; you might volunteer with an organization that offers tutoring to children in low-income neighborhoods; you might bring warm meals to homeless people in your community.

Once you've come up with an idea you can do as a group to help people and made plans on how to implement the idea, spend some time in personal reflection. During this time write on a slip of paper the names of three people you encounter on a daily or weekly basis who could use some good news and who need to know they are loved. Keep this slip with you as a reminder to show love and kindness to these people.

Wrap Up

Before you conclude, review the key points from this session:

- Perhaps no word is more important to the ministry of John Wesley and the Methodist movement than *grace*. Grace is the gift of God's love and forgiveness, made available to us without price through the life, death, and resurrection of Jesus Christ.
- Wesley understood God's grace in three movements. *Prevenient grace* is the grace at work in our lives even before we are aware of God's presence, nudging us toward a relationship with God. *Justifying grace* enables us to accept Christ and know that we are loved, saved, and forgiven. *Sanctifying grace* molds us and perfects us in God's perfect image, allowing us to be holy and to serve God and others.
- John Wesley and his friend George Whitefield ministered to coal miners outside the city of Bristol. They preached outdoors and invited thousands of people to join religious societies. These people would become the first Methodist church.
- Wesley traveled throughout England and preached thousands of sermons spreading the good news that God's grace has no limits. We can continue this work today, showing people God's grace through our witness, love, and example.

Session 5 ~April 23
Works of Mercy

My brothers and sisters, what good is it if people say they have faith but do nothing to show it? Claiming to have faith can't save anyone, can it? Imagine a brother or sister who is naked and never has enough food to eat. What if one of you said, "Go in peace! Stay warm! Have a nice meal!"? What good is it if you don't actually give them what their body needs? In the same way, faith is dead when it doesn't result in faithful activity.

Someone might claim, "You have faith and I have action." But how can I see your faith apart from your actions? Instead, I'll show you my faith by putting into practice in faithful action.

—James 2:14-18

It is estimated that John Wesley traveled more than 250,000 miles during his career. That's more than taking a trip to the moon. Wesley logged all these miles on foot, on horseback, and (in his later years) by carriage.

And instead of going to the moon, John moved about England, preaching in the streets and the markets, calling on people to submit to Christ and be born anew.

Wesley was an evangelist. The word *evangelist* is related to the word *evangelical*, and both come from the Greek word *evangelion*, which means "good message" or "good news." Evangelists are those who communicate the good news of Christ, by their words and their actions, in hopes that those who receive the message will respond by giving their lives to Christ. Evangelical Christianity is a faith focused on bringing people to Christ.

Unlike some other evangelists, John Wesley didn't see accepting Christ as a final goal but considered it a beginning. He wanted everyone to have a personal relationship with Christ but didn't want faith to stop there. Wesley saw in Scripture a call to "go on toward perfection" (Hebrews 6:1, NRSV).

Hold On, You Aren't Done Yet

Have you ever had to try out for an elite team or group—a sports team, a musical ensemble, the cast of a play, or an honor society? Preparing for an audition or tryout often requires hours of practice or conditioning. In some cases, you have to fill out forms or write essays or get letters of recommendation from teachers. The effort to make the team or get the part can be stressful and exhausting. If you're successful, you'll probably feel relieved, and you'll probably want to celebrate your accomplishment. But you won't be able to celebrate for long. The real work begins once you've earned your spot on the roster or in the cast. Perfecting your audition piece was hard work; but now you have an entire folder of new music to learn, and you have the added challenge of blending in with the rest of the band. You spent several hours writing and editing your college application essays; now that you've been accepted, you'll have to do at least that much writing and editing every week for the next four years.

The Christian life is similar. We rightfully celebrate when a person accepts God's grace and begins a new life in Christ. But we sometimes forget that this moment of rebirth is when the real work begins. Jesus Christ saves us from sin and death. But, as Paul teaches us in Ephesians 2:8-10, he also saves us for the good works that have been prepared for us. So, once we are reborn in Christ, we have a life full of good works ahead of us.

That said, there is one very important difference between accepting Christ and making the team or being accepted into college: When it comes to our relationship with Christ, we aren't the ones doing the hard work. God is doing the work through us. The good works God has prepared us for are products of God's sanctifying grace, the grace that molds us in Christ's image and pushes us on toward perfection.

Faith and Works

Almost every Christian tradition places a major emphasis on justification. Justification comes when we accept God's unconditional love and grace and begin our relationship with Christ. Often we refer to this experience as being born again. Some Christians even mark the date on which they accepted Christ and celebrate this day as a second birthday. And we should celebrate this occasion. But John Wesley would remind us that we are celebrating the beginning of something new and that we have a lifetime of growth and good works ahead of us. As we grow into the people Christ calls us to be, we are sanctified. Sanctification means to be made holy and perfected in God's love.

The Protestant Reformation put a renewed emphasis on salvation by grace through faith—not through works. As Ephesians 2:8 says, "You are saved by God's grace because of your faith." For this reason Martin Luther, whose actions were largely responsible for beginning the Reformation, didn't care for the Epistle of James. James, a short letter toward the back of the Bible, says that works are essential to our faith, that "faith without actions is dead" (see James 2:26). On the surface, James seems to contradict other New Testament epistles, which make clear that we cannot earn our salvation through what we do. But John Wesley had no trouble reconciling salvation by faith and the importance of works.

Back at Oxford, Wesley and others in his Holy Club made a habit of ministering to prisoners at the nearby Castle Prison. In Bristol, where Wesley established the first Methodist chapel, the Methodists opened the Kingswood School for the children of coal miners in the area (as well as for the children of Methodist preachers). Methodists would open many other schools to educate poor children throughout England and in the American colonies (and later the United States). Later in Wesley's life, in London, he purchased an old cannonball factory called the Foundry. At the Foundry the Methodists operated what today we would call a micro-lending program, issuing small loans to people who were starting businesses or struggling to get back on their feet. The Foundry also became a health clinic, where low-income people could come for care and to get medicine.

Jesus commands all his followers to serve people who are poor, ill, hungry, and vulnerable. (See, for example, Matthew 25:31-46.) Wesley called this outreach toward those most in need "social holiness." Social holiness is our way of participating in God's ongoing effort to fix our broken world. The Holy Spirit, through God's sanctifying grace, equips and empowers us to respond to the pain, struggle, and despair in our midst. God has worked through ordinary human beings to abolish slavery, provide relief in the wake of natural disasters, give a voice to the oppressed and neglected, and provide new opportunities to victims of conflict and abuse.

What Makes a Methodist?

John Wesley published a pamphlet titled "The Character of a Methodist" in which he explained what set apart the Methodists. They didn't have radical beliefs or unusual styles of worship. What set the Methodists apart was their complete devotion to loving and serving God and neighbor. Such devotion is a product of God's sanctifying grace.

Wesley had three rules for his Methodist societies:

1. Do no harm and avoid evil.
2. Do all the good you can.
3. Do what helps you grow in love of God.[7]

These rules seem simple, but there's a lot to them. These rules influence how we treat people, what we say, how we set our priorities, and how we manage our time. They challenge us to grow in grace through acts of love and mercy and through spiritual practices such as prayer, worship, reading Scripture, and studying Scripture.

Those of us who trace our spiritual lineage through John Wesley know that faith is not just a moment of belief. It is a lifelong commitment. When we respond to God's justifying grace and make this commitment, we'll find that God has plenty of work for us to do.

Session 5 Activities

Bible Study: James 2:14-18

Supplies: Bibles, paper, pens and pencils

What sets you apart as a Christian? Make a list of all the ways in which someone might recognize you as a Christian. Once you have a pretty good list, mark all the items that have something to do with your actions. For example, are there things that your friends and peers do that you avoid because of your faith, such as drinking or gossiping? Or are there activities that you do because of your faith, such as attending worship each week or volunteering at a food bank or nursing home?

Then make a second list, this time of other things you *could* do in response to your faith that would set you apart as a Christian. In what additional ways could you devote yourself to God? Reread the "Faith and Works" section, focusing on Wesley's thoughts on "social holiness." Consider how the Holy Spirit might be equipping and empowering you to heal the brokenness in the world.

Read James 2:14-18. Discuss:

- How, according to James, are faith and works related?
- Why do you think James says that faith without works is "dead"?
- How does this Scripture relate to John Wesley's understanding of justifying and sanctifying grace? Why did John Wesley consider actions so important to faith?

Word Study: *Sanctify*

sanctify
1. to make holy; to set apart
2. to purify
3. to revere

Reread the "Hold On, You Aren't Done Yet" section of this session. You might also want to reread "The Perfect Game" from Session 2 and "Let's Talk About Grace" from Session 4. Discuss:

- Where have you encountered the words *sanctify* and *sanctification* before?
- The word *sanctify* is related to the word *saint*. Who would you consider a saint? What makes these persons saintly?
- In what ways have you been set apart or made holy?
- How did John Wesley understand sanctification?
- Who sanctifies us? What happens to us as we are sanctified?

And Now the Real Work Begins
Supplies: Paper, pens or pencils

Let's make a couple more lists.

Think about an opportunity you've really had to work for. Perhaps you had to try out to make a team or to earn a part in a play; maybe you applied for a job or to a college. Make a list of all the things you had to do to get this opportunity.

Then, if you were successful, think about all the things you had to do once you made the team or got the job. Make a list of all the new responsibilities you had (or will have) as a result of reaching your goal.

Now compare your two lists. Which seems more difficult? Which takes more work, time, and energy?

Chances are, the items on the second list require more work, time, and energy. In some ways the Christian life mirrors making the team, getting the job, or earning the part in the play. We celebrate the moment when we accept Christ or feel an assurance of God's love and forgiveness. But once this happens, the real work begins. We spend the rest of our lives growing in grace and in love of God and neighbor. The good news is that we don't have to do all this work on our own. God's Holy Spirit is present with us, giving us the courage and the will to do all that God has prepared for us.

Micro-Lend

Supplies: Internet access

John Wesley acquired the Foundry in London as the headquarters of some of his ministries in the city. Among other things, he and the Methodists operated a lending program to assist people who were struggling financially or who were trying to get a business off the ground. This service was similar to what we know today as micro-lending programs. Most of these programs strive to assist people and communities in developing nations who are struggling financially and have limited opportunities for advancement.

As the name suggests, micro-lenders lend small amounts of money. They help people start businesses or launch projects that will benefit their communities. Unlike loan sharks, micro-lenders are not trying to profit at the expense of the people they are lending money to. Rather, they are trying to help out the borrowers and build up the communities in which the borrowers live.

Kiva Microfunds is a prominent micro-lending organization based in the United States that invites people to lend money over the Internet to borrowers in the developing world. Anyone can make a loan through Kiva, and loans can be as small as $25. Lenders can choose the project or business they would like to loan money to and can cover the entire loan or just a portion of it. Lenders through Kiva do not earn interest on their loans. The United Methodist Church's General Board of Global Ministries also allows people to finance micro-loans. They have projects in Cameroon, South Sudan, and elsewhere in the world to which people can lend money to support entrepreneurs.

As a group, select a project you can help to fund through micro-lending. You can look at opportunities through Kiva by going to www.kiva.org and choosing from one of the thousands of worthy borrowers in need of a loan. Or you can consider opportunities available through The United Methodist Church's General Board of Global Ministries. Go to www.umcmission.org/Give to Mission/Search for Projects/Advance Project Search. You could act on this information in a few different ways:

- Each member of your group could anonymously pledge to donate a certain amount of money, and you could select a loan based on your total amount.
- You could select a project you're interested in, then get the entire congregation involved. Make a presentation during worship or at another time when your congregation is meeting and tell the members of your church about the project you've selected, why you've chosen to get involved, how much money you plan on lending, and how the loan will benefit the borrowers and their communities.
- You could start a Kiva lending team at your church. Begin by setting up a team at the Kiva website. Members of the congregation would go to the website and join your church's team. They could then choose what projects they would like to finance and how much they would like to give. Members also could use the website to see how much overall money the team has lent and the impact that the team has made.

Wrap Up

Before you conclude, review the key points from this session:

- John Wesley believed in a faith that produces works. He understood that God's sanctifying grace equips us and empowers us to serve God and neighbor.
- From the beginning Methodists emphasized "social holiness" by meeting the needs of those in their midst who were poor, hungry, sick, neglected, oppressed, and vulnerable.
- John Wesley had three rules for his Methodist societies:
  1. Do no harm and avoid evil.
  2. Do all the good you can.
  3. Do what helps you grow in love of God.

Session 6 -April 30
Persevering to the End

As you do all this, you know what time it is. The hour has already come for you to wake up from your sleep. Now our salvation is nearer than when we first had faith. The night is almost over, and the day is near. So let's get rid of the actions that belong to the darkness and put on the weapons of light.

—Romans 13:11-12

Israel is the name of God's people in the Bible, and particularly the Old Testament. Even after the kingdom of Israel was sacked by the Assyrians in the eighth century B.C., prophets and writers continued using the name. Israel was actually a name given to Jacob way back in the Book of Genesis. When Jacob was on his way to meet Esau, the twin brother whom he'd betrayed, he stopped at a place called Penuel. There he ended up in a late-night wrestling match with God. Following this bout, God named Jacob "Israel," which means "one who struggles with God" (Genesis 32:22–32).

As the name "Israel" suggests, the story of God's people is a story of struggle. Throughout Scripture we encounter episodes in which God's people are unfaithful, act recklessly, and put God to the test. Through it all, God never gives up on them. And, in the ultimate act of redemption, we see God live among people in the person of Jesus, enduring human suffering, dying, and then defeating death to atone for the sins of humanity and to give us hope for eternal life.

God is still among us, in the person of the Holy Spirit, doing the work of redemption. Our world is broken—marred by death, despair, disease, and destruction. While we see examples from Scripture and from history in which God delivers entire nations and heals whole communities, much of God's work of redemption and revival happens one individual at a time. Each one of us has a part to play.

Wake Up

John Wesley felt as though many Christians of his day had fallen into a spiritual sleep and needed to be revived. He saw people who might be described as "sleepwalking"—going through the motions of being a Christian without fully devoting themselves to Christ. For the most part these Christians knew what God had saved them *from* but were less concerned with what God had saved them *for*.

John Wesley knew that, for many years, he had called himself a Christian but had been asleep spiritually. He had been baptized, educated in theology, and ordained as a priest. He had been the leader of a "Holy Club" at Oxford. He had crossed the Atlantic in hopes of bringing new people to Christ. But even after all this, Wesley had not truly experienced God's love in his life. He had not yet wakened to God's grace.

Wesley's day job was as a teacher and tutor at Oxford. This afforded him the opportunity to preach in many different churches throughout England. To each one, Wesley brought his message of awakening. Plenty of people—both laypeople and other priests—who heard Wesley preach found his message unnerving or even offensive. These people were comfortable in their faith and didn't like being told they were "sleepy." They weren't interested in hearing that being a Christian involved more than just believing in Jesus and not being as bad as the average person.

Eventually these churches got sick of Wesley preaching in their pulpits and stopped inviting him back. So, as he had done in Bristol, Wesley took to the streets. On many occasions, bullies interrupted these street sermons in hopes of getting Wesley to stop or driving him out of town. John Wesley wrote in his journal about one such incident at Market Cross in Bolton, England, in 1748:

> At one I went to the cross in Bolton. There was a vast number of people, but many of them utterly wild. As soon as I began speaking, they began thrusting to and fro, endeavoring to throw me down from the steps on which I stood. They did so once or twice, but I went up again and continued my discourse. They then began to throw stones; at the same time some got upon the cross behind me to push me down.[8]

This sort of adversity became routine to John Wesley. He was beaten and hit with rocks, and homes where he stayed were set ablaze. But none of these setbacks kept him from preaching.

Rocking the Boat

When John Wesley was in his sixties, he decided to speak out against slavery. Slavery was not widespread in Wesley's England, but British merchants and ships facilitated the slave trade elsewhere, such as in the American colonies. Bristol, the city in southwest England where John Wesley founded the first Methodist chapel, was a major hub for these merchants. Ships would leave Bristol for eastern Africa, where traders would purchase slaves before transporting them to the American colonies. Wesley published a widely read pamphlet denouncing slavery and England's role in it.

Many of the Methodists in Bristol relied on the slave trade for a living. So in 1788 when Wesley preached a sermon at Bristol's New Room chapel condemning slavery, things got uncomfortable. Wesley, who was nearly eighty-five at the time, wrote about the incident in his journal: "The people rushed upon each other with the utmost violence, the benches were broke in pieces, and nine-tenths of the congregation appeared to be struck with the same panic."[9] A fight broke out in the chapel between those who supported slavery and those who were against it.

Methodism Settles Down

Methodist preachers have never been prone to settling down. The first Methodist societies were small groups that met in homes. John Wesley went from church to church, preaching to anyone who would have him, and later preached in the streets. Still today, ordained pastors in The United Methodist Church commit to itinerancy, meaning that they may be moved from one congregation to another as determined by a bishop.

As the Methodist movement grew, it became necessary to establish chapels where Methodists could meet for prayer, Bible study, and worship. During Wesley's latter years, hundreds of Methodist chapels popped up in England. (Remember, again, that these new Methodist churches were a part of the Church of England.) In 1778 Wesley opened a new Methodist chapel in London, called City Road Chapel, across from where his mother Susanna was buried. John Wesley lived in the house next door to this chapel until he died in 1791. The congregation at City Road Chapel, now called Wesley's Chapel, remains active today.

John Wesley noticed, as Methodism became more established, that there were many wealthy people in the Methodist churches. This hadn't been the case when the movement began. Wesley worried that prosperity would distract people from their relationship with Christ. He cited 1 Timothy 6:9: "But people who are trying to get rich fall into temptation. They are trapped by many stupid and harmful passions that plunge people into ruin and destruction." To address this issue, Wesley introduced three rules to inform a Christian's use of money: First, gain or earn all you can. John Wesley saw nothing wrong with earning money, provided no one got hurt in the process. Second, save all you can. Wesley warned Methodists not to spend their money frivolously but to be wise with their investments. He especially advised them against making unnecessary purchases for the purpose of impressing others. Third, give all you can. Wesley wanted everyone in his churches to provide for themselves and their families. Once that was accomplished, Wesley taught, they should give their money to those who could not meet their own needs.[10]

According to legend, John Wesley earned thirty pounds during the first year of his ministry. He lived off of twenty-eight and gave away two. Before long his salary increased to sixty pounds. Since he was capable of living on twenty-eight pounds per year, he did. And he was able to give away thirty-two pounds. Wesley's salary continued to increase, but he was always able to live on twenty-eight pounds. By the end of his career, he was donating about ninety percent of his total earnings.

"I'll Praise My Maker While I've Breath"

Wesley continued preaching well into his eighties. He died at the age of eighty-seven, an especially old age considering that the life expectancy in eighteenth-century England was in the thirties.[11] Elizabeth Ritchie, John Wesley's friend and housekeeper, was with him when he died. She reported that, shortly before his death, Wesley tried to sing the hymn "I'll Praise My Maker While I've Breath," by Isaac Watts. It begins, "I'll praise my Maker while I've breath; and when my voice is lost in death, praise shall employ my nobler powers."[12]

During his long career, John Wesley preached to hundreds of thousands of people (and possibly more) in England and the American colonies. Over and over again, he asked his audience whether they were asleep or awake, whether they were aware of their sin and need of a Savior, whether they knew about God's love for them, and whether they wanted to grow in their relationship with God and others. Those of us today who call ourselves Christian should continue John Wesley's revival by asking these questions of ourselves and others.

Session 6 Activities

Bible Study: Romans 13:11-12

Supplies: Bibles, phones or other devices with alarm clocks

Find out who in your group uses an alarm clock and what type of alarm clock they use. Have anyone who uses an alarm on their phone or other electronic device play the alarm they wake up to. They should explain why they chose that particular noise or song. What is it about this particular sound that helps them get up in the morning?

Then read aloud Romans 13:11-12. These verses are from a letter the Apostle Paul wrote to the Christians in Rome. Discuss:

- What do you think Paul means when he tells the Roman Christians to "wake up" from their sleep?
- What do you think Paul means when he refers to "the day" that is near? (You might compare these verses to another passage from one of Paul's letters, 1 Thessalonians 5:1-11.)
- What are "actions that belong to the darkness"?
- What are "weapons of light"?

Many of us have alarms that wake us up in the morning. Think about some spiritual alarms. What wakes you from your spiritual sleep and helps you focus on your relationship with Christ?

Ask the members of the group to identify one spiritual alarm they can set in the coming weeks. Such an alarm might take the form of regular conversations about faith with a friend or mentor, a commitment to be present for worship every Sunday, or a Bible verse posted on your mirror or in your locker as a daily reminder of who you are and whom you belong to.

Word Study: *Awaken*
Supplies: Bibles, a markerboard or large sheet of paper, markers

awaken
1. to wake up
2. to stop sleeping

When we use the word *awaken*, we are often referring to sleep. But sleep is not the only state from which we wake up. As a group, make a list on a markerboard or large sheet of paper of other things from which one can wake up. (For instance, a person might wake up from an addiction or a misguided way of thinking.) For each item on the list, talk about how one's life would change after "waking up" from that state.

Reread Romans 13:11-12 and the "Wake Up" section from this session. Discuss:

*   What do these texts tell us about waking up?
*   What can we do to wake ourselves spiritually?
*   What can we do to stay awake?

Going Through the Motions
Supplies: Simple percussion instruments (optional)

Select a familiar song that everyone in your group knows. It could be a current pop song; it could be a song that your group sings on retreats or at other events. As a group, sing through the song, first with little energy or enthusiasm. Then sing through it again, this time loudly and with excitement. The second time through, you might clap your hands or keep time with simple percussion instruments. After singing the song twice, discuss:

*   When is your faith like the first time through the song, bland and lethargic? Why might your faith lack energy at these times?

- When is your faith like the second time through the song, enthusiastic and full of life? Where does this spiritual energy come from?
- What spiritual practices keep your energy level up?

Divide the group into pairs or groups of three. In each smaller group the partners should discuss ways in which they will stay spiritually alert during the coming weeks.

Take a Stand

Supplies: A markerboard or large sheet of paper, markers, Internet access on at least three devices, paper, pens or pencils

Reread the "Rocking the Boat" section of this session.

Late in his life, John Wesley took a stand against the slave trade. He saw an injustice and decided to do something about it. The slave trade had a global reach. It was a lucrative industry that had the backing of some of the world's most powerful governments. No individual person had the power or influence to bring down the slavery industry. When slavery eventually was abolished, no single person could take credit. Rather, it took the effort and influence of a large number of people over many decades. Yet each individual contribution was crucial.

On a markerboard or large sheet of paper, make a list of issues today that have a national or global impact and that threaten the lives or well-being of many people. Focus especially on issues that seem much too big for any individual to address. Once you have a pretty good list, go through each item and identify at least one way that an individual young person could respond to this problem or injustice.

Then, as a group, select one of the issues on your list. Divide your group into three teams. (If you have a small number in your group, one or more of the teams may have only one or two people.)

- One team should look at how the church is already responding to the issue you chose.
- One team should look at ways governments (local, state, and national, as well as governments of other nations) are already responding to the issue.
- One team should look at ways that businesses and other organizations are already responding to the issue.

Have each team spend ten or fifteen minutes doing research. Then each team can report on what it has learned. Following these reports, discuss how your entire group could respond to your chosen issue. Consider ways you could work with ministries and organizations that are already making a difference. Look into what they need and what volunteer opportunities are available. Come up with a plan that is specific, timely (something that can be done in the coming week or month), and measurable (something that can be evaluated to determine whether it has been successful and whether you might do things differently). Since you will be doing this work as representatives of your congregation, be sure to tell your pastoral staff about the plan and keep them informed.

Make sure to follow through on your plan, and assign roles to different people in the group. One person could have the responsibility of running the idea by the pastoral staff; one could have the job of making contact with organizations you would like to partner with; one person could take on the task of doing additional research to get a better understanding of the issues and needs involved. Check with one another every few days to make sure the plan is progressing.

The Money Rules

Supplies: Bibles, posterboard or large sheets of paper, assorted art supplies

As Methodists became more prosperous, John Wesley became concerned. He didn't want the love of money to pull people away from their faith. So he came up with three rules regarding money:

1. Gain all you can.
2. Save all you can.
3. Give all you can.

Read aloud each of the following Scriptures. Discuss how each one relates to Wesley's rules and how Christians use money.

- Matthew 6:24
- Luke 12:13-21
- Luke 21:1-4
- 2 Corinthians 9:10
- 1 Timothy 6:10

Wesley's rules on wealth are as relevant today as they were in the 1700s. Teach these rules to your congregation by making a poster. Include all three rules, with illustrations, as well as some of the Bible verses listed above or others that relate to the use of money.

Ask permission to place your poster somewhere in the church building where much of the congregation will see it.

Wrap Up

Before you conclude, review the key points from this session:

- John Wesley called people to wake up spiritually by surrendering their lives to Christ and by making a habit of spiritual practices.
- Wesley's message wasn't always popular. His sermons made a lot of people defensive and uncomfortable.
- In his old age, Wesley took a strong stand against the slave trade.
- Wesley had three rules for the use of money: Gain all you can; save all your can; give all you can.

Notes

1. Holland Nimmons McTyeire, *A History of Methodism: Comprising a View of the Rise of This Revival of Spiritual Religion in the First Half of the Eighteenth Century, and of the Principal Agents by Whom It Was Promoted in Europe and America* (1884; Nashville: Publishing House of the Methodist Episcopal Church, South, 1919), 41.

2. Kevin Rudy, "The Odds of Throwing a Perfect Game" (http://blog.minitab .com/blog/the-statistics-game/the-odds-of-throwing-a-perfect-game).

3. John Wesley journal entry for June 22, 1736. From *The Works of John Wesley, Volume 18*, ed. W. Reginald Ward and Richard P. Heitzenrater (Nashville: Abingdon Press, 1988), 228.

4. U.S. Department of Commerce, Bureau of the Census, Geography Division. "Census and You." Washington, DC: U.S. Department of Commerce, Bureau of the Census, Geography Division, 1993.

5. John Wesley journal entry for May 24, 1738. From *The Works of John Wesley, Volume 18*, 249-250.

6. Richard P. Heitzenrater, *Wesley and the People Called Methodists*, 2nd ed. (Nashville: Abingdon, 2013), 110.

7. See "The Nature, Design, and General Rules of the United Societies" (1743) in *The Works of John Wesley, Volume 9*, ed. Rupert Davies (Nashville: Abingdon Press, 1989), 70–73.

8. John Wesley journal entry for August 28, 1748. From *The Works of John Wesley, Volume 20*, ed. W. Reginald Ward and Richard P. Heitzenrater (Nashville: Abingdon Press, 1991), 245.

9. John Wesley journal entry for March 3, 1788. From *The Works of John Wesley, Volume 24*, ed. W. Reginald Ward and Richard P. Heitzenrater (Nashville: Abingdon Press, 2003), 70.

10. See John Wesley's sermon "The Use of Money" (1760), in *The Works of John Wesley, Volume 2*, ed. Albert C. Outler (Nashville: Abingdon Press, 1985), 268–280.

11. Oded Galor and Omer Moav, "Natural Selection and the Evolution of Life Expectancy" (Nov. 17, 2005), 3-4 (http://sticerd.lse.ac.uk/seminarpapers/dg09102006.pdf).

12. "I'll Praise My Maker While I've Breath," *The United Methodist Hymnal* (Nashville: United Methodist Publishing House, 1989), 60.